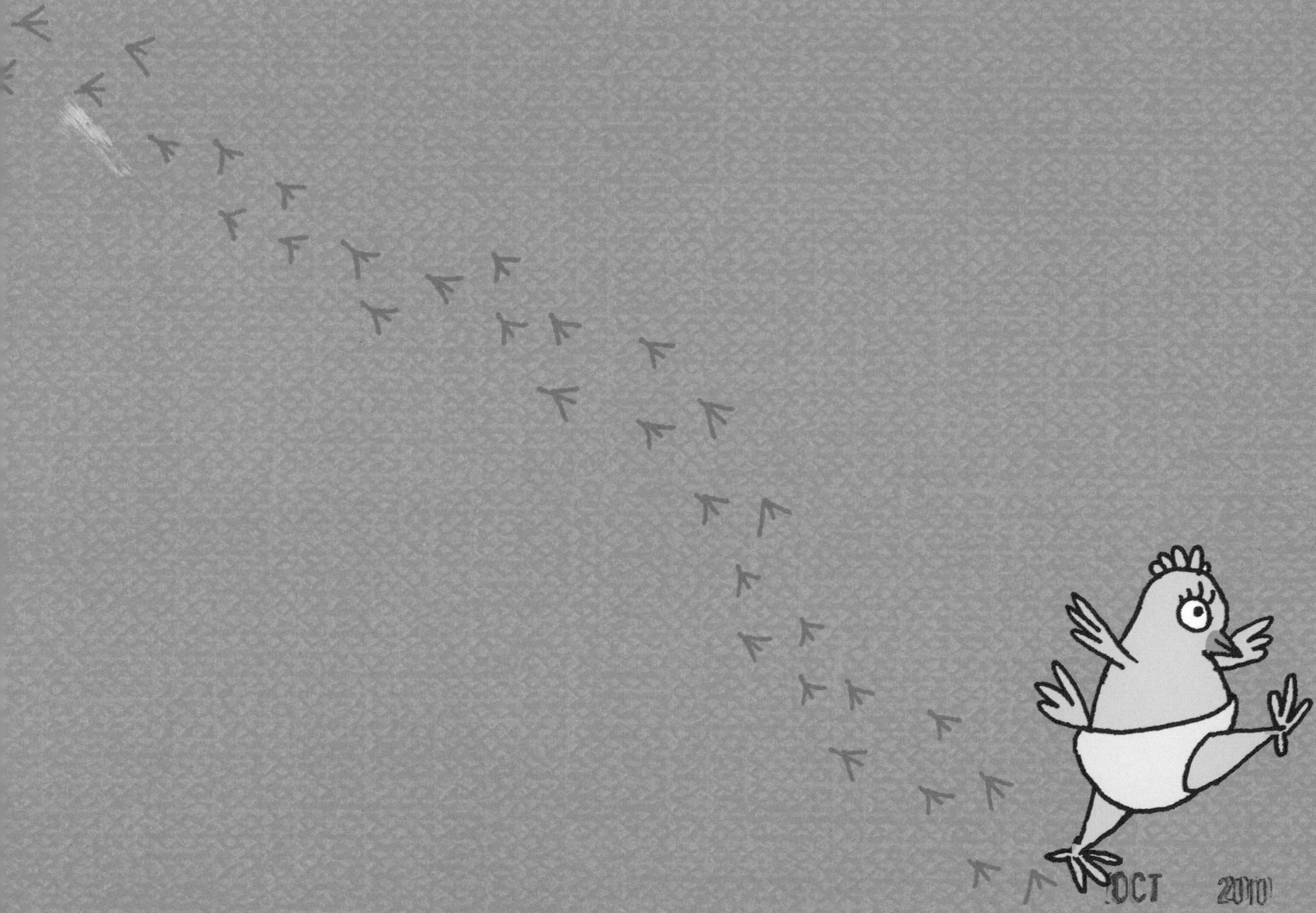

Book design by Amelia May Anderson.
Typeset in American Typewriter, Zirconia, Souper Sans,
and Noodle Script.
The illustrations in this book were rendered in pen and
colored digitally.

Library of Congress Cataloging-in-Publication Data
Shannon, George.
Chicken scratches : Grade A poultry poetry and rooster rhymes /
by George Shannon & Lynn Brunelle ; illustrated by Scott Menchin.
p. cm.
ISBN 978-0-8118-6648-4
1. Chickens—Juvenile poetry. I. Brunelle, Lynn. II. Title.
PS3569.H335C47 2010
811'.54—dc22
2009028987

Manufactured by Toppan Leefung, Da Ling Shan Town,
Dongguan, China, in November 2009.

10 9 8 7 6 5 4 3 2 1

This product conforms to CPSIA 2008.

Chronicle Books LLC
680 Second Street
San Francisco, California 94107

www.chroniclekids.com

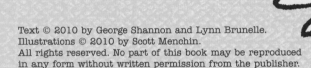

CHICKEN SCRATCHES

GRADE A — POULTRY POETRY AND ROOSTER RHYMES

By George Shannon & Lynn Brunelle

Illustrated by Scott Menchin

chronicle books · san francisco

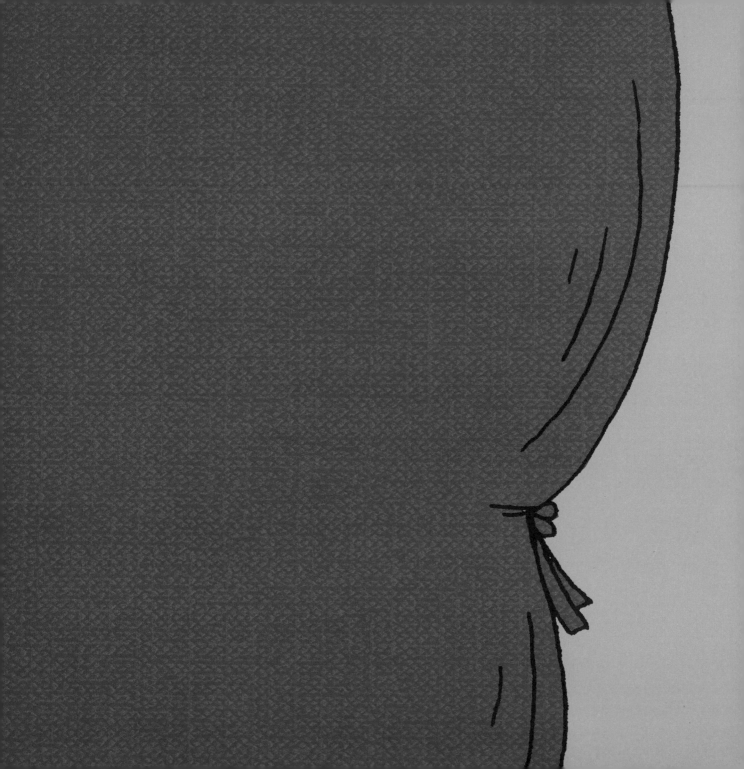

BALLET OLÉ

A chicken named *Millicent Smites*
loved to twirl and *leap* to new heights.
 Till one night on her toes,
as she danced with a rose,

she laid a fresh egg in her tights.

FIRST STEPS

Chickie STEP.

Chickie **boom.**

Chickie chickie STEP STEP.

Chickie chickie boom.

TEETER

totter

Chickie chickie STEP STEP boom.

Chickie chickie STEP STEP STEP then

BOOM.

STEP
STEP STEP
Chickie chickie STEP STEP!

Chickie chickie *quickie* chickie zoom zoom zoom!

Gr-ouch

There was a special chicken,
though she was quite a grouch.
She laid square eggs and talked a lot,
but all she said was, "OUCH!"

SICK DAY

The day the rooster had the flu
he could not cock-a-doodle-do.
He could not walk. He could not talk.
No one was sure just *what* to do.
They called a doctor to the coop,
who brought a bowl of chicken soup.
"Drink up," he said. "It's good for you.
I promise it's no one you knew."

HALLOWEEN

Not last night, but the night before,
three little chicks came peeping at my door.
One was a **DEVILED** egg. Two were **SWEETS**.
And all three yelled out,

"TRICK

or TREAT."

Hula Zelda

Hula Zelda was a dancer.
Brother! Could she shimmy!

UP
and
down,
she'd twist *around*

and *wiggle* every limb-y.

She put the *WOW* in luau
as she *hula*-ed through each night.

And when she clucked ALOHA
roosters crowed in sheer delight.

She loved the island rhythms
so much it sometimes hurt.
'Cause every egg that Zelda laid
came wearing a *grass skirt*.

IN CONCERT

Hildegard, my chicken pal,
sang as sweet as a root canal.
Now she's hit the opera stage.
Her shocking sounds are all the rage.

We sing her praises every day
as long as she sings far away.

wishbone

Make a Wish

You think a wishbone is lucky?
Just make a wish and snap it?!
My wishbone's lucky tucked inside,
where nobody can crack it!

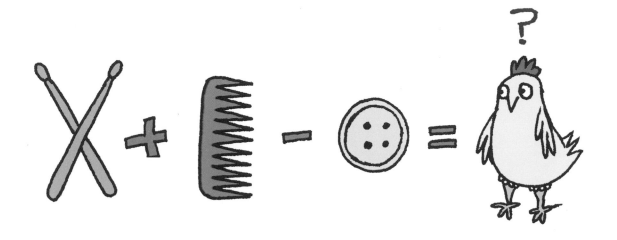

MISmatch

I'm sure you've heard the many facts
that make the chicken rare.
It has two drumsticks and a comb,
yet neither drum nor hair.
It even has a belly,
but there is no button there!

Pocket Money

Henny Penny, penny-pincher,
kept a penny in her purse.
But when she took her penny out,
her day turned bad, then worse.

Someone **pinched** her,
then her penny,

LAUGHED, and ran *away*.

"Stop!" she clucked. "That penny's saved until a rainy day!"

She ran to catch the pinching thief, and **WHACKED** him with her purse.

Then good old Henny Penny *pinched her penny in reverse!*

Tug-o-Worm

One worm.
Two chicks.
Worm won.
Fiddlesticks!

Watch What
You Eat

A chicken ate a pack of seeds
before she read the label.
Next day she laid a cantaloupe
upon the breakfast table.

TIME TRAVELER

We chickens are a time trip,
we're visions from the past—
we're living, breathing relatives
of creatures long, long past.

My feathers, wings, and scaly feet
have ancient tales to tell
of Stegosaurus, Allosaurus,
locked inside each cell.

See the Archaeopteryx
emerging as I soar?
Listen to my cluck and hear
Tyrannosaurus roar!

Supersaurus, Hadrosaur,
Agilosaurus, too.
Velociraptor, Troodon,
the whole Jurassic crew.

All that dino DNA
lives in my family tree.
Want to see a dinosaur?
Just take a look at me!

Yummy in My Tummy Bugs

Sing a song of tasty bugs.
Snacks to **CRUNCH** and munch.
Crisp and *roly-poly* bugs
to scratch up for my lunch.

Sing a song of *slimy* slugs.
Treats to **CHOMP** and chew.
Sweet and *slinky-shrinky* slugs
to snatch and *slurp* their *goo!*

Champion

Chickie Teriyaki,
a sumo superstar,
tossed his weight around the ring
and bumped opponents far.

His shape was very ovular.
His wrestling suit was small.
So when he bowed to start a match,
fans nearly saw it all!

RECESS

There are chickens on the playground,
but none are satisfied.
They must keep running back and forth
to reach the other slide.